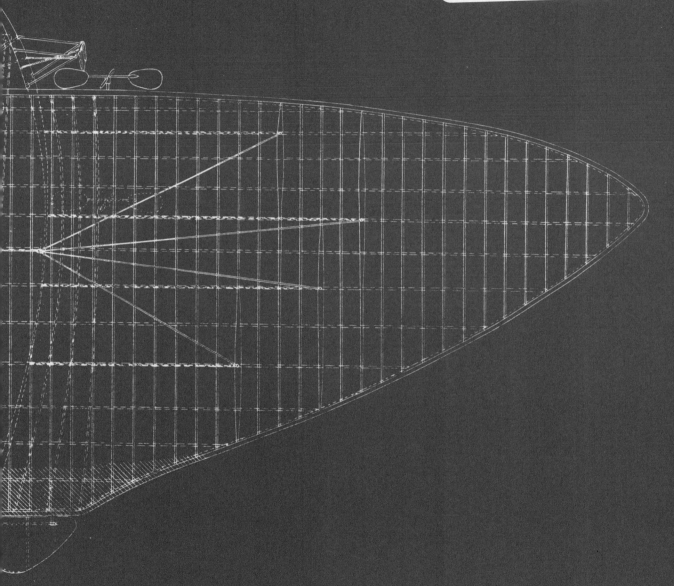

Early Flying Machines

1799-1909

Early Flying Machines

1799-1909

Charles Gibbs-Smith

Eyre Methuen London

PICTUREFILE

First published 1975
by Eyre Methuen Ltd
11 New Fetter Lane, EC4P 4EE
© 1975 Charles Gibbs-Smith
Printed in Great Britain by
Butler & Tanner Ltd
Frome and London

ISBN 413 33020 6

Introduction

This is an international portrait gallery of early flying machines: many of the subjects never took to the air they were designed to fly in; but many more did manage to leave the ground, especially after 1900. It is not a history of early aviation; but the illustrations do cover many of the noble and ignoble failures, and most of the successes partial or complete.

Modern aviation started with Sir George Cayley, who initiated the modern fixed-wing aeroplane configuration, and laid down the basis of the science of aerodynamics between 1799 and 1809. He built both models and full-scale machines, from 1804 onwards, and tested them with varying degrees of success. He was indeed the 'Father of Aerial Navigation' in every sense of the word.

Throughout the nineteenth century, it was the lack of a light and powerful engine – the steam engine was too heavy except for models – which thwarted the inventors' efforts to take to the air; but this lack also undoubtedly saved many necks by keeping the more foolish or conceited firmly on the ground. Ballooning (started in 1783) and parachute jumping (started in 1797) also helped keep alive air-mindedness during the century-long incubation period, which had to precede the conquest of the air in 1903–8. In the nineteenth century there was also a prodigious amount of wasted effort, as well as valuable work done by the pioneers; but lack of proper communication also made it difficult for the individual inventors to know what was happening, and to proceed in an orderly and progressive way.

In the first half of the century, apart from Cayley's work, the one bright star was the brilliantly prophetic design for a monoplane in 1842–3 by W. S. Henson, called the *Aerial Steam Carriage*, which was only built in unsuccessful model form, but illustrations of which were spread over the world for more than half a century.

In 1848, Henson's engine-builder, John Stringfellow, built a steam-driven model of his own which almost, but not quite, sustained itself in the air. There was also an important oddity, the first published tandem-wing design by Thomas Walker in 1831, which helped to inspire Brown and Langley in years to come.

In the 1850s, probably inspired by Henson, a number of paper designs for full-scale aircraft appeared in Europe such as Michel Loup's in 1853, and Félix Du Temple's in 1857; the latter's model, about this time, was the first model aeroplane to fly under its own power. In 1858–9 F. H. Wenham carried out his important tests on aerofoils (published 1866–7) which showed that a cambered wing derives most of its lift from the front portion; hence a long narrow wing was the best weight-lifter.

The descendants of those brave but foolhardy tower-jumpers of old, who fixed artificial wings to themselves and jumped into space, still persisted, but in a new form; for Louis Letur killed himself in 1854 when descending in his curious parachute-type glider. In 1858 J. M. Le Bris attempted to fly in his glider based on the Albatross.

The 1860s saw many more professional and mechanically-minded men take up aviation; and the first aeronautical societies were also founded in France (1863) and Britain (1866). Wenham read to the Aeronautical Society, in that year, his influential paper advocating high-aspect ratio wings. There was also much activity in France, where the first proper design for a jet plane was produced in 1865 by Charles de Louvrié, but not built. In 1867 the Englishmen J. W. Butler and E. Edwards designed their jet and propeller-propelled delta-wing machines, also not built. In 1868 The Aeronautical Society staged the world's first aero-exhibition at the Crystal Palace in which appeared Stringfellow's steam-powered model triplane; this, although it could not fly, exerted much influence on those who came later, and inspired the modern biplane and triplane

configurations. As a tailpiece to the 1860s, it must be recorded that Lenoir in France invented the gas engine in 1860, which was ultimately to lead to the petrol engine of today.

The elastic-powered model aeroplane arrived in the 1870s, of which the most significant was Alphonse Pénaud's 'Planophore' of 1871, also the first model in France to incorporate inherent stability long after Cayley had built his own first model in 1804: this little model of Pénaud's exerted great influence on pioneers thereafter. The decade also saw the first wind-tunnel, built by Wenham and Brown in 1871; and experiments by D. S. Brown with tandem-wing model gliders (1873–4), which probably influenced Langley, and certainly inspired Hargrave in Australia to invent the box-kite. In 1874 the Belgian Vincent de Groof was killed in his curious ornithoptering parachute. About 1874, Du Temple's full-scale powered plane ran down a ramp, took off, but could not fly. Thomas Moy built and tested his compressed-air-driven model monoplane in 1879, which powerfully reinforced Henson's inspiration. Again a tailpiece to the decade, and again about engines; for the German N. A. Otto achieved the practical four-stroke petrol engine in 1876.

Aeronautical activity in the 1880s saw a slight lull; but Horatio Phillips published his model aerofoil sections in 1884, which were the first to demonstrate what Cayley suspected, i.e. that the bulk of the lift on a cambered aerofoil is obtained from negative pressure on the upper surface rather than positive pressure beneath: this discovery had a profound influence on the later pioneers. Also in 1884 came a creditable effort by the Russian, Alexander Mozhaiski, to test his steam-driven full-scale monoplane, piloted by I. N. Golubev: it ran down a ramp and took off, but could not fly.

Of the utmost future importance to aviation was the world's first automobile, built by Carl Benz in 1885, quickly followed by the Daimler. Aviation was later to call heavily on the personnel of the motor car industry both for its engineers and its pilots.

As the last decade of the century arrived, the enlightened men realised that the powered aeroplane could not be a long way off. The inventors seemed naturally to split into two main streams; there were the 'chauffeurs' who looked upon the aeroplane as a sort of winged automobile, to be driven off the earth and guided about the sky; and the true 'airmen' who looked upon the aircraft as an extension of their own bodies. To the latter, flight control was the all-important achievement, and gliders the machines which must be mastered before going on to powered aircraft. To the 'chauffeurs' flight-control was of minimal importance, and they sought to drive their machines into the air by brute force: it was a lucky thing that they did not succeed.

In 1890 Clément Ader, a famous French engineer, managed just to take off in his steam-powered *École*, but the machine could not be sustained or controlled, and could not fly. In 1894, Sir Hiram Maxim – of Maxim gun fame – built and tested a giant biplane test-rig which just managed to lift itself clear of the rails on which it ran; but that too could not fly, and was abandoned. Next came the American scientist S. P. Langley with his tandem-wing steam-powered models which flew successfully in 1896. He was later (1903) to build and test a full-scale machine. Then, in 1897 Ader, with a bigger but no better machine, the *Avion III*, attempted to fly it on two occasions; but it never flew for an instant. Later on, Ader was to claim mendaciously that it had flown for 300 metres, and it was not until the official report was published in 1910 that the world knew that he had lied.

The giant of the second half of the century was a true airman, who, by his brilliant pioneering work with gliders, inspired and precipitated single-handed the final phase in the conquest of the air. He was a German engineer, Otto Lilienthal, who from 1891 to 1896 (when he was killed flying) designed and constructed a number of hang-gliders, including three biplanes; in these machines he was suspended by his arms, and swung his torso and legs in any desired direction to shift the centre of gravity, and thus exercise a limited amount of flight-control. Lilienthal was the first man in history to get up into the air and fly properly in gliders: his influence was widespread and profound; he summed up the aspirations of the century behind him, and pointed the immediate way to triumph ahead.

A follower of Lilienthal's, and the only man who might have beaten the Wright brothers in the race to fly, was the Scottish engineer Percy Pilcher; he had progressed rapidly in the flying of hang-gliders by 1896, and in 1899 had already built the engine for his proposed powered machine, when he, too, was killed gliding on his *Hawk*.

Far away in Australia was an isolated inventor of prime quality, Lawrence Hargrave, and his contribution was of vital importance: for in 1893 he invented the box-kite, which he first published in the same year, and examples of which he brought to Europe in 1899: this kite was to provide the Europeans with a new and successful conception of inherent stability, which – from 1905 onwards – formed the basis of the standard Voisin aeroplanes of 1908–10.

Two vitally important propagandists of aviation broadcast, as widely as possible, accurate information about the history of flying. The first of these men was an eminent American civil engineer, Octave Chanute, who in 1894 published the first accurate history of aviation, *Progress in Flying Machines*. He then went on to make an

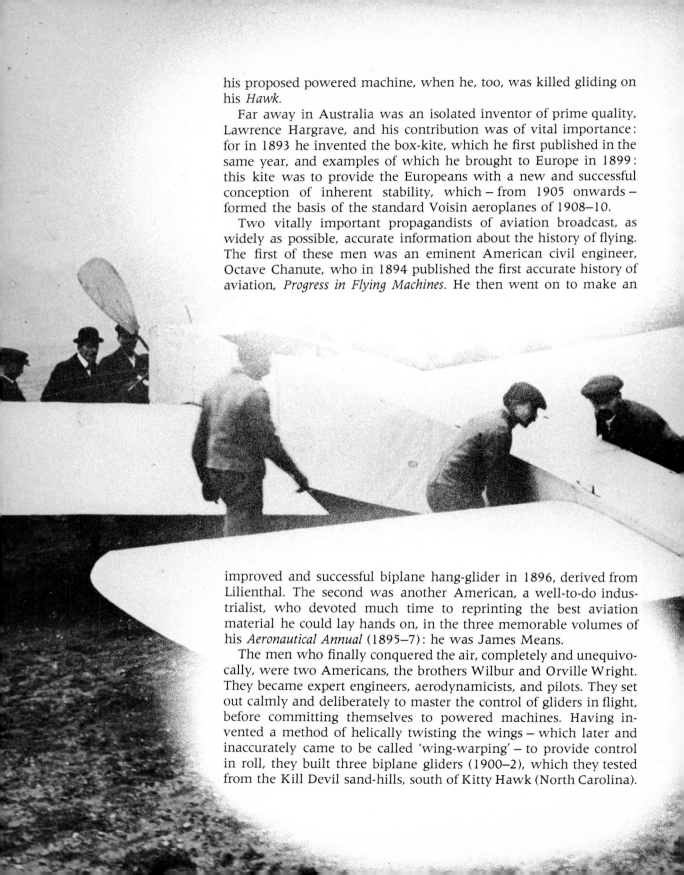

improved and successful biplane hang-glider in 1896, derived from Lilienthal. The second was another American, a well-to-do industrialist, who devoted much time to reprinting the best aviation material he could lay hands on, in the three memorable volumes of his *Aeronautical Annual* (1895–7): he was James Means.

The men who finally conquered the air, completely and unequivocally, were two Americans, the brothers Wilbur and Orville Wright. They became expert engineers, aerodynamicists, and pilots. They set out calmly and deliberately to master the control of gliders in flight, before committing themselves to powered machines. Having invented a method of helically twisting the wings – which later and inaccurately came to be called 'wing-warping' – to provide control in roll, they built three biplane gliders (1900–2), which they tested from the Kill Devil sand-hills, south of Kitty Hawk (North Carolina).

The pivotal machine was the third (1902), which was first fitted with twin fixed rear fins, which were then exchanged for a single movable rear rudder in order to counteract the warp-drag of the wings, and allow the pilot to achieve both safe banked turns, and to level up the wings if they were gusted out of the horizontal. Thus, for the first time in history, the problem of full three-axis control was effectively solved. From this properly controllable glider No. 3 of 1902, all flight-control of modern aircraft derives directly.

Langley had been commissioned by the US Government to build a full-scale tandem monoplane, which he called – with scant respect for etymology – An *Aerodrome*. Piloted by Manly, this machine was twice launched from a houseboat on the River Potomac in 1903, and plunged into the river on both occasions, having fouled the launching gear. Despite his supporters' claims, the Langley *Aerodrome* would not have been successful, as it incorporated severe faults of various kinds. It was then abandoned.

In 1903 the Wrights were building their first powered *Flyer*. This machine not only incorporated three-axis control, but two other features also entirely conceived and constructed by the brothers: the 12 h.p. petrol engine, and then the excellent airscrews, which were the first to be geared down in relation to the engine revolutions, and hence to provide optimum thrust. On 17 December 1903, at the Kill Devil Hills – and from level ground – the Wrights made the world's first four powered, sustained, and controlled flights in an aeroplane.

During 1904 and 1905 in their second and third *Flyers* – the name they gave to all their powered machines – the brothers went on to perfect their invention. In their *Flyer III* of 1905, they solved the outstanding aerodynamic problems, and then could with ease perform circles and figures-of-eight, and remain airborne for over half an hour at a time: this Wright *Flyer III* was the world's first fully practical powered aeroplane, and its all-round performance was not to be equalled by any other aircraft in the world – apart from later Wright machines – until 1909.

Aviation in Europe, after the death of Lilienthal in 1896, went into a profound decline. Apart from the ambitious but unsuccessful seaplane of the Austrian Wilhelm Kress (1901), the only man who kept Continental aviation alive was the French Captain Ferdinand Ferber, who had first tried to imitate a Lilienthal glider; then in 1902 he learnt from Chanute about the Wrights' gliding, and immediately abandoned his Lilienthal-type machine and started to imitate the Wright types in 1902–4. The entire revival of European aviation was due to these primitive copies of Wright gliders by Ferber, and to subsequent Wright-type gliders built by Ernest Archdeacon and Robert Esnault-Pelterie (1904–5), which Chanute had inspired after he lectured on the Wrights in Paris in April of 1903.

Then, in 1904, Ferber made a major contribution by adding a

stabilising fixed tailplane to the Wright biplane-form he had adopted, and thus revived the favourite European idea of a stable machine: this move of Ferber's formed the beginning of the practical European biplane tradition. In 1905 the Hargrave box-kite was combined with the Wright biplane-configuration (with forward elevator) in order to produce a safe stable machine. The man responsible for this marriage was Gabriel Voisin, with the assistance of his two clients, Archdeacon and Louis Blériot: he produced two float-gliders which were towed off the Seine by a motor boat; neither was successful but they were nevertheless the immediate ancestors of the stable European biplanes.

At this time, the Europeans unwisely abandoned gliders and the mastery of flight-control, with the result that the development of their aviation was greatly slowed down. Then, at the end of 1905, a powerful and effective spur was applied: this was the detailed news of the Wrights' power-flying from 1903 to 1905, especially their triumphant 1905 season with the *Flyer III*: this news was officially published by the famous journal *L'Aérophile*, the organ of the Aéro-Club de France. It was the anger and resentment created by this revelation of the Wrights' achievements which finally sparked the Europeans into productive activity in powered aviation.

Owing especially to the refusal of the Europeans to master glider flight before venturing on powered aeroplanes, along with the inexplicable delay and confusion they suffered, the progress of European flying continued to be slow, although there were now signs of progress following the news of the Wrights, a progress which would start to gather momentum through 1906 and 1907.

At last, in September and October 1906, the Brazilian Alberto Santos-Dumont – who had turned from airships to aeroplanes after hearing about the Wrights – made the first official hop-flights in Europe on his outlandish canard ('tail first') biplane *14-bis* at Paris, the best of which lasted only 21.1/5th seconds, and covered only 721 ft. Also in 1906, there appeared the machine which started the European monoplane tradition; built by the French-domiciled Transylvanian, Trajan Vuia, it was unsuccessful in itself, but exerted great influence on the pioneers to come.

It was not until March 1907 that the first powered descendant of the Voisin float-gliders – the Voisin-Delagrange biplane – was airborne for 6 seconds, its best time ever; and not until November of this year that Wilbur Wright's flight of 59 seconds in 1903 was just exceeded by Henri Farman, flying another Voisin. On 13 January 1908, Farman made the first official circle in Europe; but by August, European flying was still in only a primitive stage, with little or no ability to manoeuvre.

Wilbur Wright, on his new standard biplane, first flew in public in August 1908, near Le Mans (France), and continued to perform brilliantly there throughout the year, making many flights of over an hour, and one of $2\frac{1}{2}$ hours, as well as many passenger flights. This 'revolution' was primarily a revelation of perfect flight-control, with the machine being banked, turned, circled, and flown in figures of eight, with the greatest of ease; and secondly, a revelation of propulsion technology, as the Wright airscrews were geared down to rotate at optimum speed, and produce maximum thrust for minimum power; whereas all the European propellers rotated at engine speed, and thus too fast to 'grip' the air. But it was Wilbur's brilliant flight-control – especially in roll combined with control in yaw – that taught the Europeans the one great lesson they needed. Having learned their lessons, it took little more than a year for Europe to rival the Wrights, and three years to overtake them.

The first European fully to grasp the Wrights' 'message' was Henri Farman, who first fitted large effective ailerons to his much-modified Voisin machine in the Autumn of 1908: with these in place, he made the world's first cross-country flight, followed closely by Blériot in another cross-country achievement.

It was the remarkable aero-engine built by Leon Levavasseur which might almost be said to have made European aviation possible; these engines were named Antoinette – after his chief's daughter – and the 8-cylinder 50 h.p. motor was fitted to countless European aeroplanes during the 1906–9 period.

The year 1909 marked a decisive stage in the history of aviation; for in that year, having learnt from the Wrights, the Europeans staged two events of epoch-making significance. One was Louis Blériot's crossing of the English Channel in his frail No. XI, on 25 July. The other was the first of the world's great aviation meetings, held in August on the Plain of Betheny, outside Reims: of the 38 machines which were entered, 23 were airborne, and 87 flights of over 3 miles were achieved: the distance record was set up by Henri Farman, who flew 112 miles in just over 3 hours: the fastest speed was some 46–7 m.p.h.

Farman was the popular 'hero' of Reims: he was technically an Englishman – he became a naturalised Frenchman in 1937 – being the son of British parents living in France. After using, and constantly modifying, a Voisin biplane since 1907, he designed his own first biplane early this year (1909); it was called the *Henry Farman III*, and – with its numerous progeny – this elegant machine became one of the classic aircraft of history.

Particularly important was the fact that there were six machines at the Reims meeting – four biplanes and two monoplanes – which were practical and reliable, and were on sale to the public.

With the Reims meeting, the aeroplane had finally 'arrived': it was now looked upon as the latest of the world's practical vehicles, albeit a somewhat dangerous – but exciting – one.

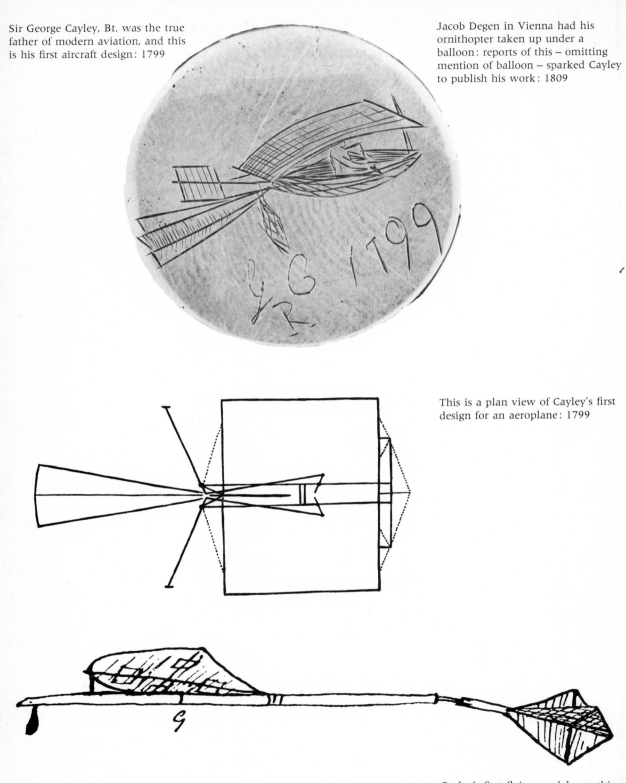

Sir George Cayley, Bt. was the true father of modern aviation, and this is his first aircraft design: 1799

Jacob Degen in Vienna had his ornithopter taken up under a balloon: reports of this – omitting mention of balloon – sparked Cayley to publish his work: 1809

This is a plan view of Cayley's first design for an aeroplane: 1799

Cayley's first flying model was this glider with a kite up front and a cruciform tail-unit behind: 1804

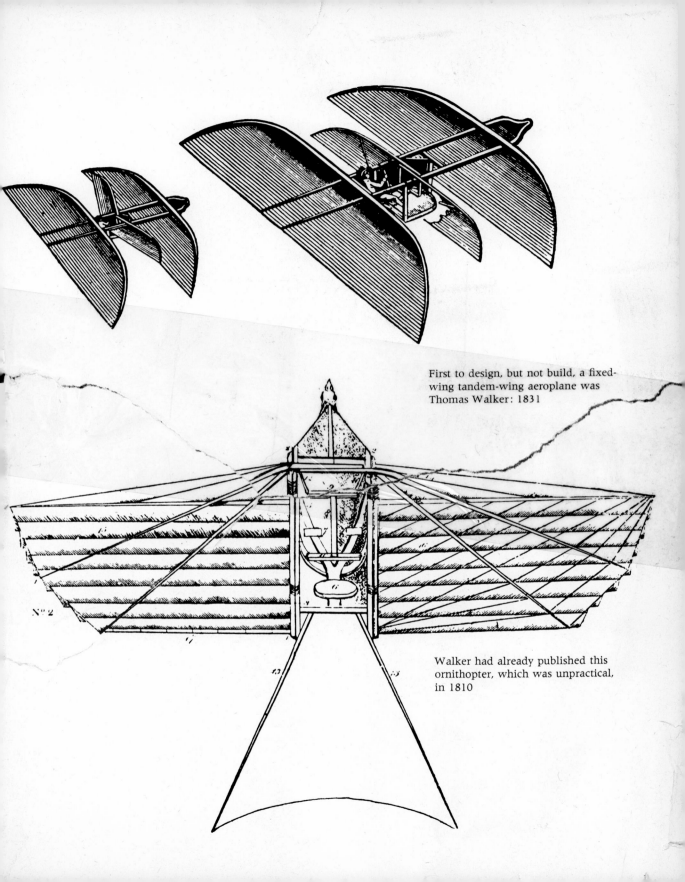

First to design, but not build, a fixed-wing tandem-wing aeroplane was Thomas Walker: 1831

Walker had already published this ornithopter, which was unpractical, in 1810

VOL A TIRE D'AILES
Exécuté pour la 1ere fois à Paris dans le Jardin de Tivoli
Par Mr DEGEN, Mécanicien de Vienne en Autriche.
Le 10 Juin 1812.

Gravé sur verre et Imprimé par Guérry.

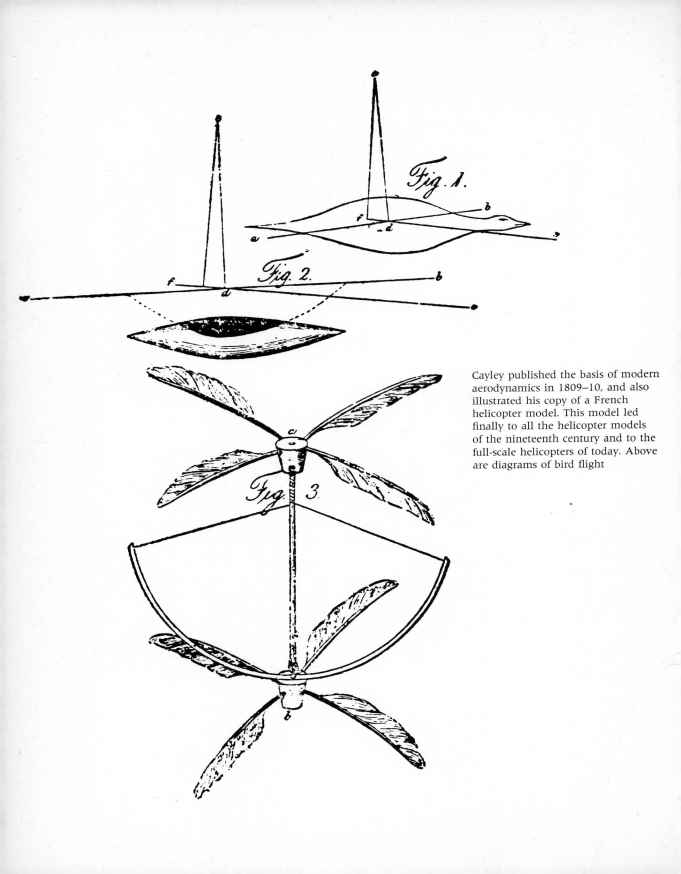

Fig. 1.

Fig. 2.

Fig. 3.

Cayley published the basis of modern aerodynamics in 1809–10, and also illustrated his copy of a French helicopter model. This model led finally to all the helicopter models of the nineteenth century and to the full-scale helicopters of today. Above are diagrams of bird flight

Englishman W. S. Henson published
this prophetic design for a monoplane
in 1843: it influenced many inventors
thereafter, and was repeatedly
re-published all over the world. The
machine was never built in full scale

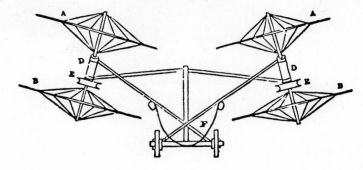

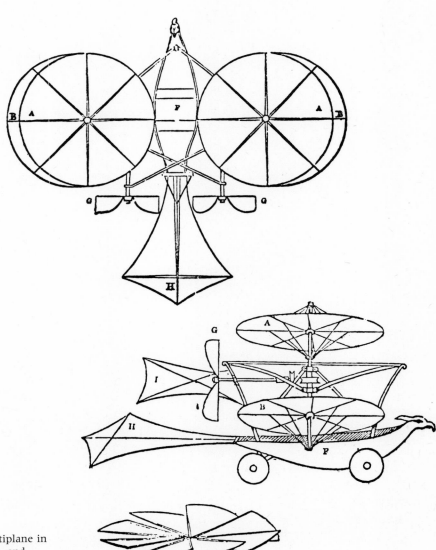

Cayley designed this convertiplane in
1843, to helicopter upwards, and
then fly horizontally

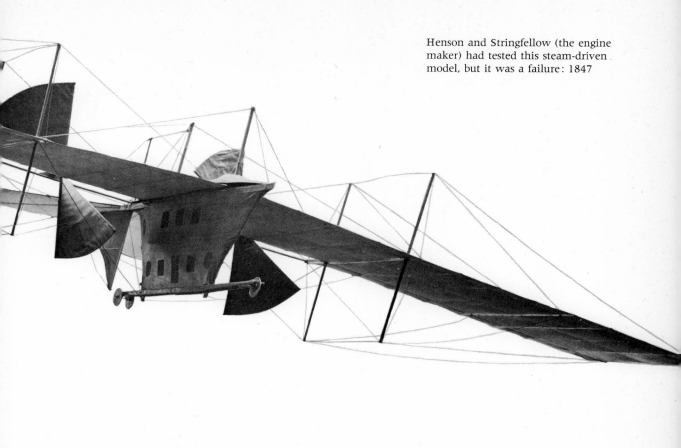

Henson and Stringfellow (the engine maker) had tested this steam-driven model, but it was a failure: 1847

Henson abandoned aviation, leaving John Stringfellow to build and test this steam-driven model, which almost flew, in 1848. Stringfellow then waited until 1868 before he reappeared

Cayley designed, built, and flew this
triplane as a glider in 1849, with
either ballast or a boy on board, for
brief periods

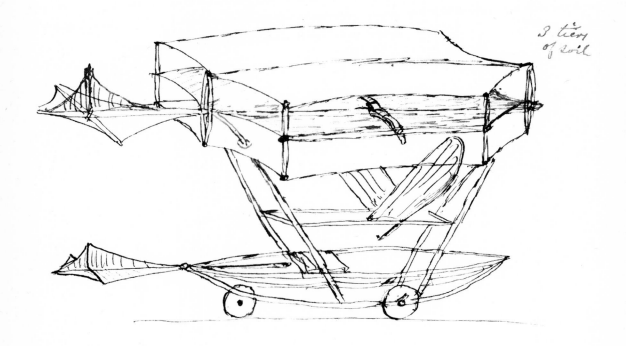

3 tiers
of soil

In 1852 Cayley published this
prophetic design for a glider; but
it was never built. It had an
adjustable tail-unit, along with
combined elevator and rudder

𝕸𝖊𝖈𝖍𝖆𝖓𝖎𝖈𝖘' 𝕸𝖆𝖌𝖆𝖟𝖎𝖓𝖊,

MUSEUM, REGISTER, JOURNAL, AND GAZETTE.

No. 1520.]   SATURDAY, SEPTEMBER 25, 1852.   [Price 3*d*., Stamped 4*d*.

Edited by J. C. Robertson, 166, Fleet-street.

SIR GEORGE CAYLEY'S GOVERNABLE PARACHUTES.

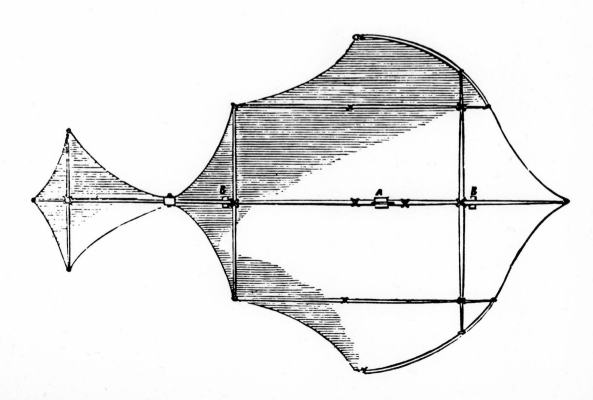

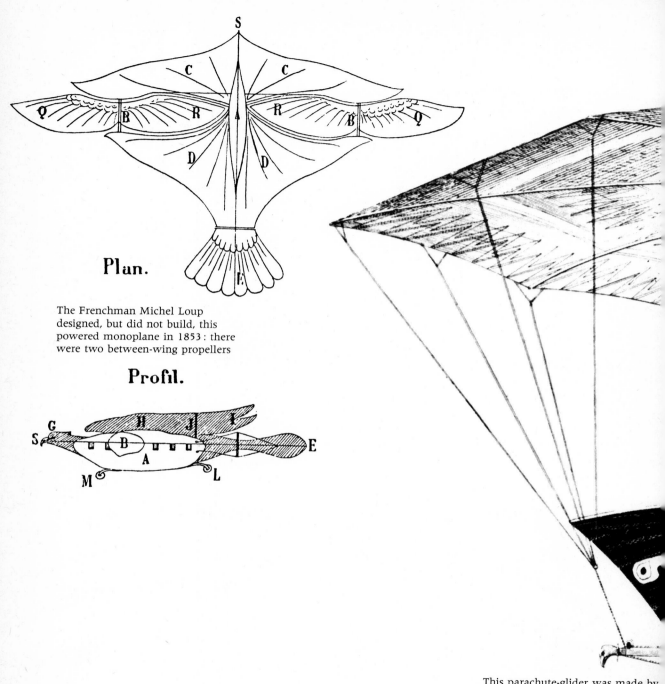

S

C C

Q B R A R B Q

D D

E

Plan.

The Frenchman Michel Loup
designed, but did not build, this
powered monoplane in 1853: there
were two between-wing propellers

Profil.

G H J I
S B E
A
M L

This parachute-glider was made by
the Frenchman L. Letur and dropp[e]
from a balloon in 1853–4. When
being taken up he was dragged ove[r]
trees and killed: 1854

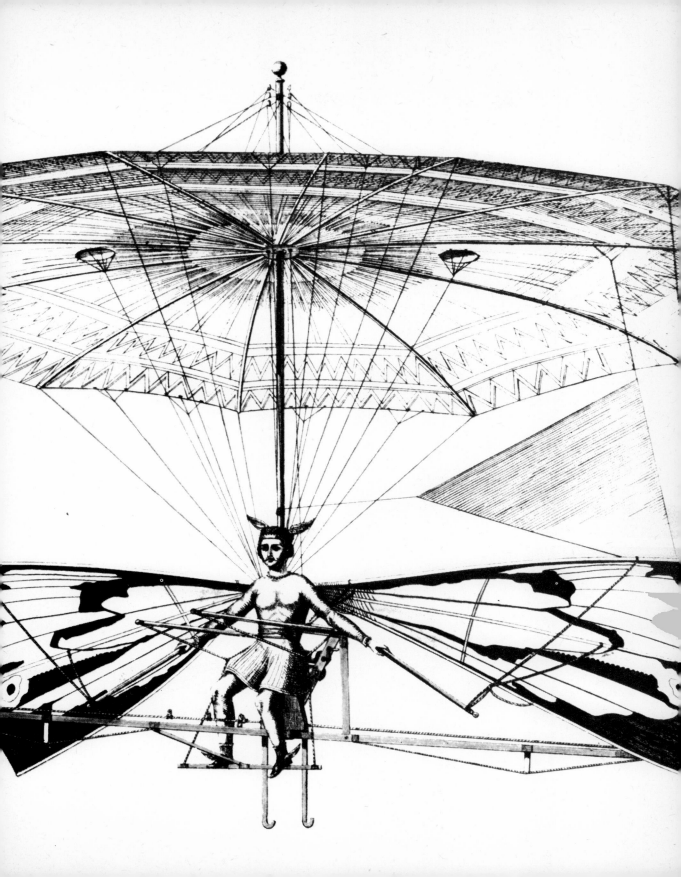

This is the remarkable design
patented in 1857 for a powered
monoplane by the Frenchman Félix
Du Temple. A model, thought to
have been similar to this, was the
world's first powered model to
sustain itself in the air, about
1857–8. Du Temple was later to
build a full-scale machine (see
page 33)

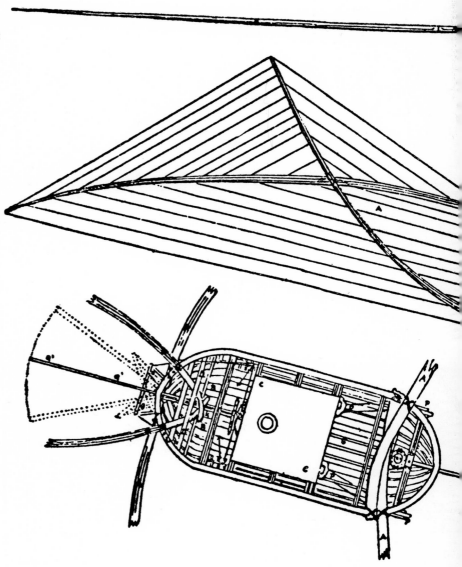

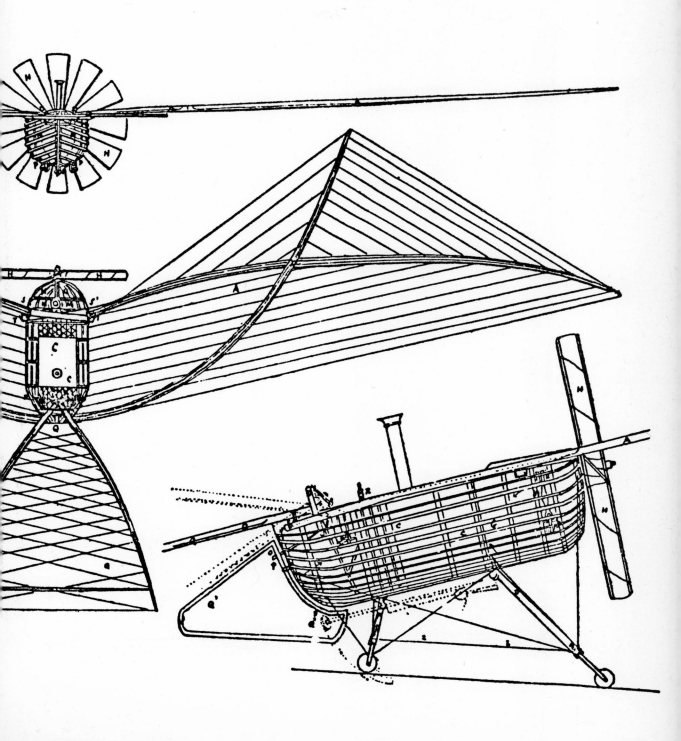

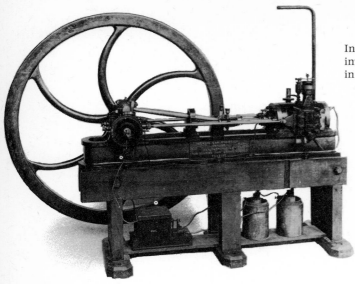

In 1860, the Frenchman Lenoir invented the gas engine, a vital step in prime movers

The world's first jet aeroplane was designed, but not built, by the Frenchman de Louvrié, in 1865

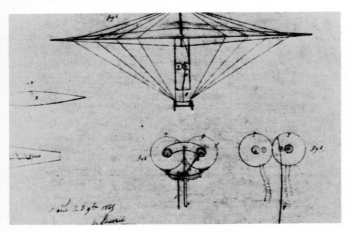

In 1866, Wenham published proof that a high aspect-ratio wing produced the most lift

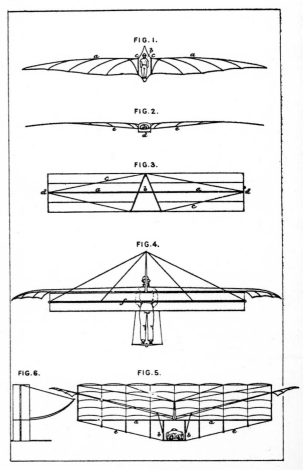

FIG. 1.

FIG. 2.

FIG. 3.

FIG. 4.

FIG. 6.

FIG. 5.

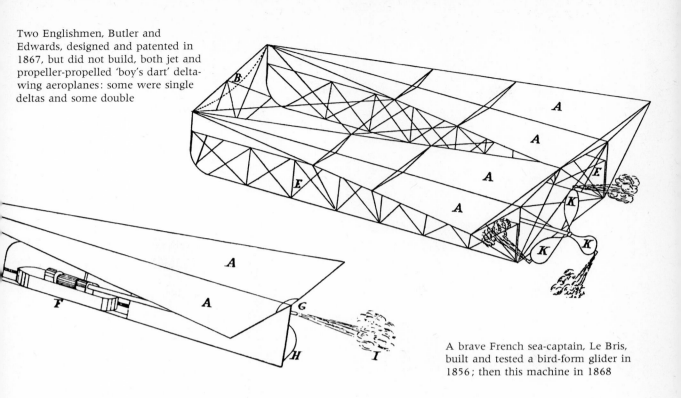

Two Englishmen, Butler and Edwards, designed and patented in 1867, but did not build, both jet and propeller-propelled 'boy's dart' delta-wing aeroplanes: some were single deltas and some double

A brave French sea-captain, Le Bris, built and tested a bird-form glider in 1856; then this machine in 1868

Prelude to the Farnborough Air
Show! In 1868 was the first air show
in history, at the Crystal Palace

In 1868 John Stringfellow re-emerged
and with this unsuccessful triplane
model, which inspired many later
inventors to use super-posed wings,
including biplanes

This romantic monster was designed,
but never built, by Kaufmann, but a
model was exhibited in 1868

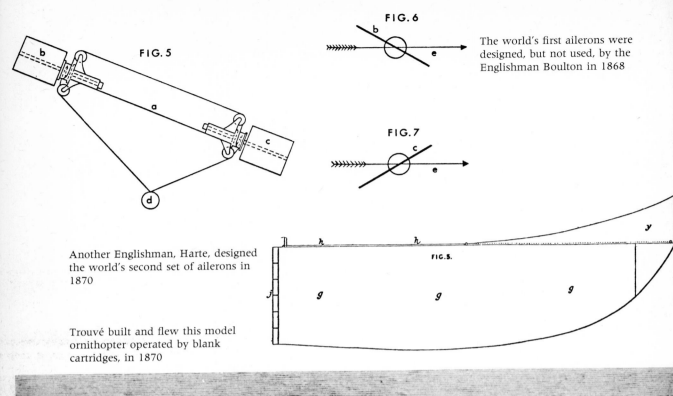

FIG. 5

FIG. 6

FIG. 7

The world's first ailerons were designed, but not used, by the Englishman Boulton in 1868

FIG.S.

Another Englishman, Harte, designed the world's second set of ailerons in 1870

Trouvé built and flew this model ornithopter operated by blank cartridges, in 1870

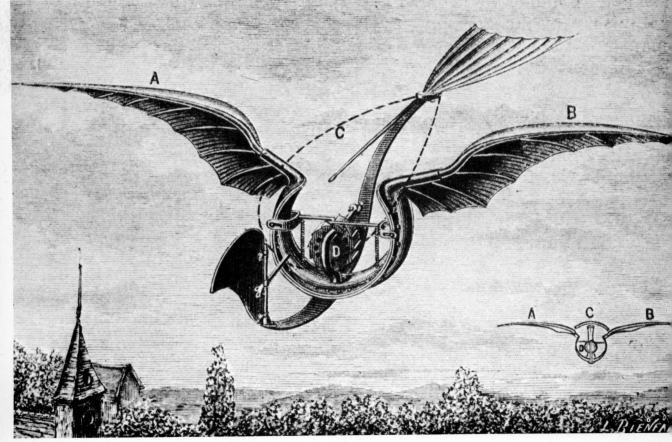

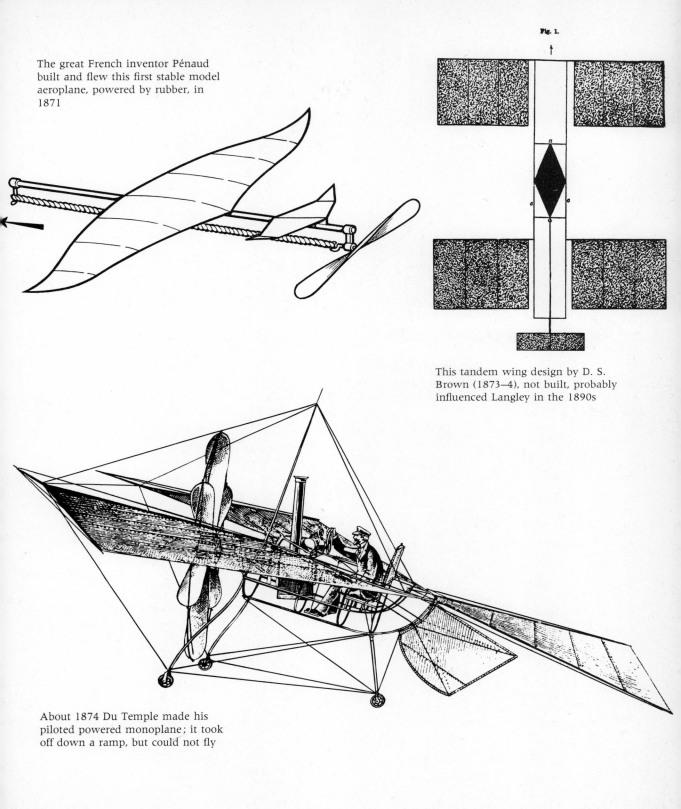

The great French inventor Pénaud
built and flew this first stable model
aeroplane, powered by rubber, in
1871

Fig. 1.

This tandem wing design by D. S.
Brown (1873–4), not built, probably
influenced Langley in the 1890s

About 1874 Du Temple made his
piloted powered monoplane; it took
off down a ramp, but could not fly

A large steam-driven tandem-wing
model monoplane tested by Thomas
Moy in 1875

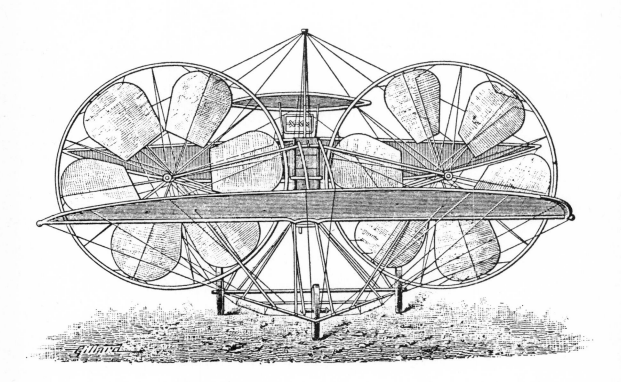

The Belgian De Groof plunging to
his death in his semi-ornithopter
in 1874

Pénaud's design, with help from
Gauchot, for a twin-propellered
monoplane, patented in 1876, but
never built. This remarkable machine
had a glass-domed cockpit, single
control column, a retractable
undercarriage, and was to be
amphibious into the bargain. It
was to have twin elevators, rear fin
and rudder, and Pénaud even
thought of fitting proper flight
instruments. It was one of the most
sophisticated and advanced
conceptions of the nineteenth
century

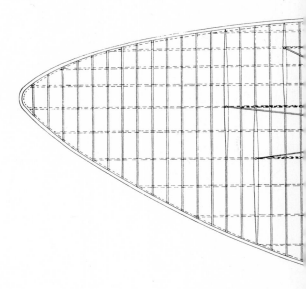

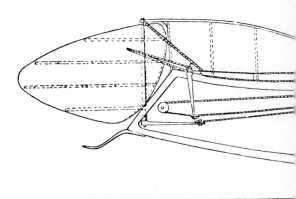

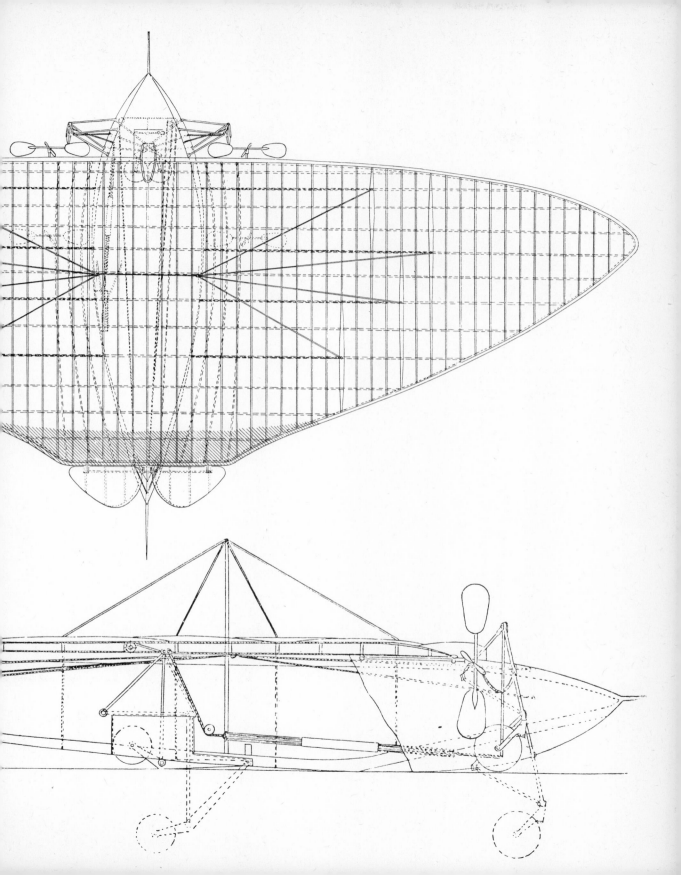

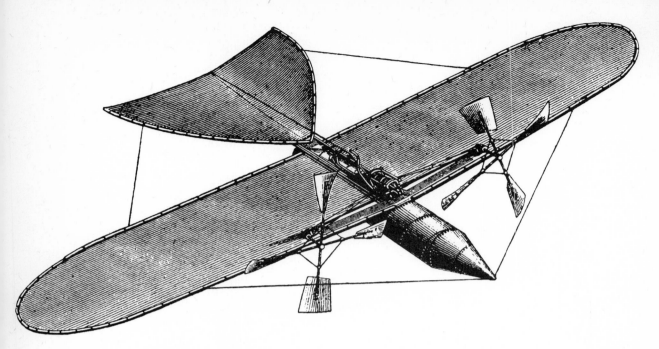

The model, powered by compressed
air, flown by Tatin in 1879

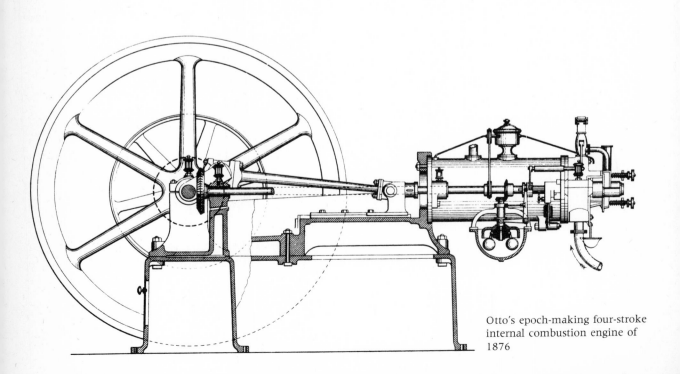

Otto's epoch-making four-stroke
internal combustion engine of
1876

In 1884 Phillips patented these wing-sections; he was the first man to demonstrate that a properly curved double-surfaced aerofoil provides much more lift above the top surface by negative pressure, than on the underside of the aerofoil by positive pressure; another epoch-making discovery

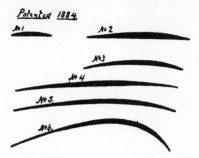

Mozhaiski's powered monoplane in Russia, which failed to fly, about 1884

Benz in Germany built the first petrol automobile in 1885

Jules Verne encouraged air-
mindedness by his aerial romances
(this is in 1886)

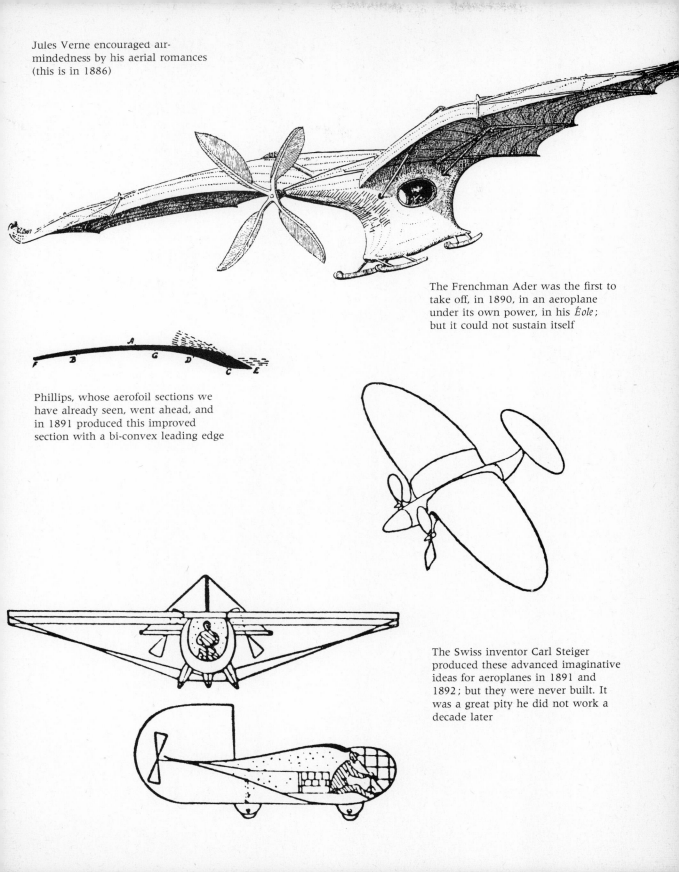

The Frenchman Ader was the first to
take off, in 1890, in an aeroplane
under its own power, in his *Éole*;
but it could not sustain itself

Phillips, whose aerofoil sections we
have already seen, went ahead, and
in 1891 produced this improved
section with a bi-convex leading edge

The Swiss inventor Carl Steiger
produced these advanced imaginative
ideas for aeroplanes in 1891 and
1892; but they were never built. It
was a great pity he did not work a
decade later

In 1893 Phillips, of aerofoil fame, tested this multi-slat-wing model at Harrow

Sir Hiram Maxim built and tested, with only minor success, this giant steam-driven biplane test-rig in 1894

In 1893 Hargrave in Australia
invented the box-kite, which has
remained a popular form of kite

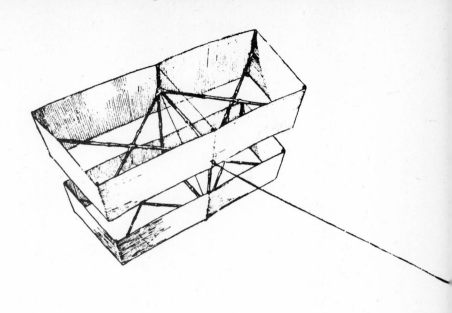

The German Otto Lilienthal was the greatest aviation pioneer of the latter half of the century. He built and flew gliders and made hundreds of excellent glides between 1891 and 1896. He hung in his gliders, and swung his body and legs to shift the centre of gravity and exercise some measure of flight-control

Lilienthal made both monoplane and biplane gliders, and also made an artificial hill from which he could launch himself into the wind. Here we are looking up at one of his biplanes, with a fine view of the structure of the wings

A fine view, from the rear, of one of his biplanes. Lilienthal did not use any movable control surfaces, but he was experimenting with them at the end of his life. Unfortunately he was killed in one of his monoplane gliders in 1896. But his influence on those pioneers who came after was immense, and included the inspiration of the Wright brothers

One of the great pioneers was the
American Octave Chanute, who
produced this glider in 1896

In 1896, the American scientist
Langley achieved some success with
this, and one other, tandem-wing
steam-driven model

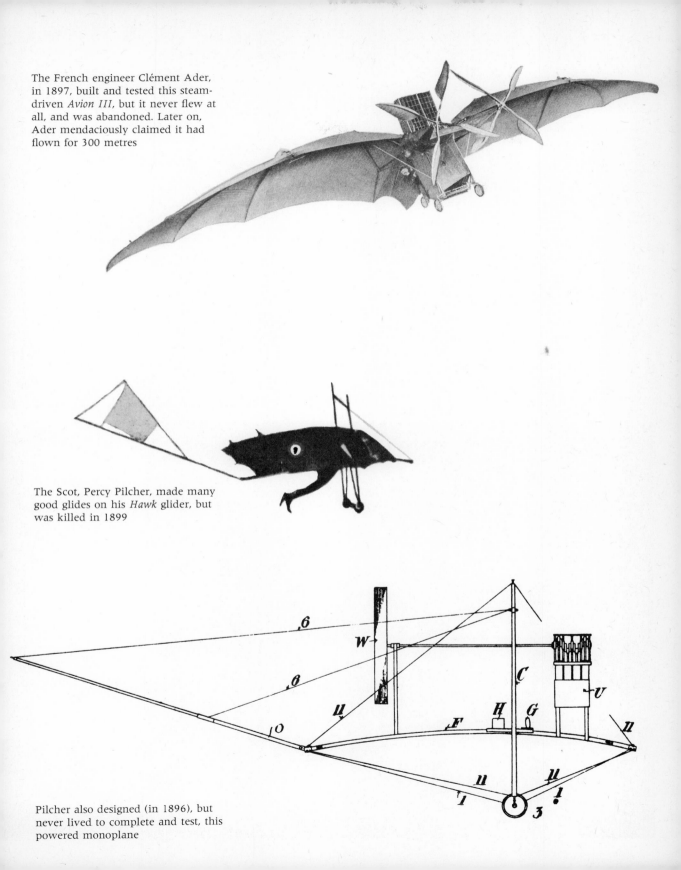

The French engineer Clément Ader, in 1897, built and tested this steam-driven *Avion III*, but it never flew at all, and was abandoned. Later on, Ader mendaciously claimed it had flown for 300 metres

The Scot, Percy Pilcher, made many good glides on his *Hawk* glider, but was killed in 1899

Pilcher also designed (in 1896), but never lived to complete and test, this powered monoplane

In 1899 the Wright brothers, Wilbur and Orville, entered aviation with this biplane kite, whose wings could be 'warped' to make it bank, or to right it. In 1900 they flew their first man-carrying glider at Kitty Hawk, with wing-warping and front elevator. This was the start of modern aviation

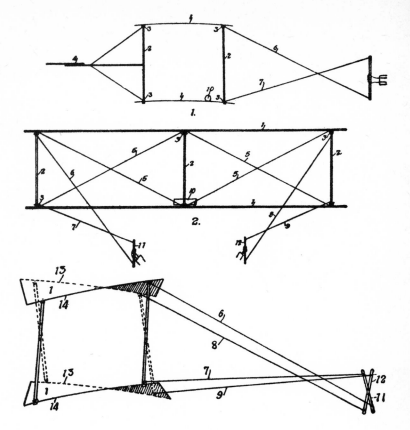

Before building a full-scale *Aerodrome*
(as it was misnamed), Langley flew
this quarter-scale petrol-driven model
in 1901

This flying-boat, built by the Austrian
Kress, was destroyed in 1901 before
testing

The Wright brothers, satisfied with the preliminary results of their kite and glider tests, built and flew this new man-carrying glider at the Kill Devil Hills in 1901. It did not come up to their expectations; so they reworked their calculations and started again, to design a third glider [left]

With this glider of 1902, in its second version with a rear rudder instead of the double fixed fin, the Wrights mastered the secret of full three-axis flight control, *i.e.* control in pitch, yaw and roll, by means of the elevator, the rudder and the warping of the wings. It was flown at the Kill Devil Hills, near Kitty Hawk, North Carolina. All modern aeroplanes derived their control systems from this truly epoch-making glider

An enterprising German, Jatho, failed to fly in 1903, in this powered aeronautical oddity

Captain Ferber, in France, started making crude copies of a Wright glider in 1902, and thus re-started European aviation

In 1903, Ferber was still trying to fly
Wright-type gliders, but they were so
crude that he had little success

S. P. Langley completed and tested
(in 1903) his full-scale piloted
Aerodrome (so-called); and twice had
it launched from a house-boat on
the Potomac, in October and

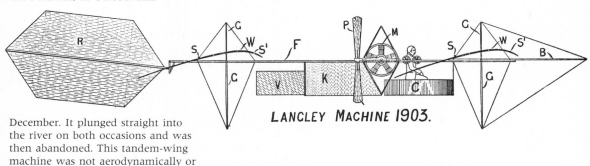

LANGLEY MACHINE 1903.

December. It plunged straight into
the river on both occasions and was
then abandoned. This tandem-wing
machine was not aerodynamically or
structurally sound, and it would
never have flown properly

After having mastered the flight-control of gliders, the Wrights turned to powered flying, and in 1903 had completed their first engined *Flyer*, which, on 17 December 1903, made the world's first powered, sustained and controlled flights at the Kill Devil Hills, near Kitty Hawk, North Carolina. The longest flight of four lasted for 59 seconds, covering 852 feet, a feat not rivalled in Europe until the end of 1907. This is the first flight which lasted for 12 seconds. The Wrights designed and built the aircraft, the engine, and the propellers

Esnault-Pelterie tried out ailerons on
this 1904 glider, but the machine
was unsuccessful

In 1904 the Europeans were
struggling ineffectually with their
primitive Wright-type gliders. The
Archdeacon glider

In 1904 Ferber fitted a stabilising tail
to his glider

In 1904 the Wrights successfully flew
their second powered biplane, which
could circle and fly for five minutes.
This was flown near their home town
Dayton

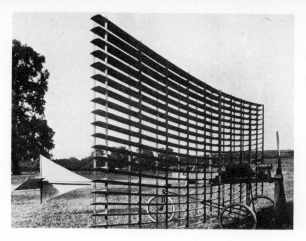

Phillips reappeared with this unsuccessful slat-wing aeroplane in 1904

Archdeacon tests his second glider in 1905, which is unsuccessful and crashes

Gabriel Voisin built two float gliders in 1905, based on Hargrave's box-kite, one for Archdeacon and one for Blériot [right]. Both were towed off the Seine by a motorboat, and both were unsuccessful

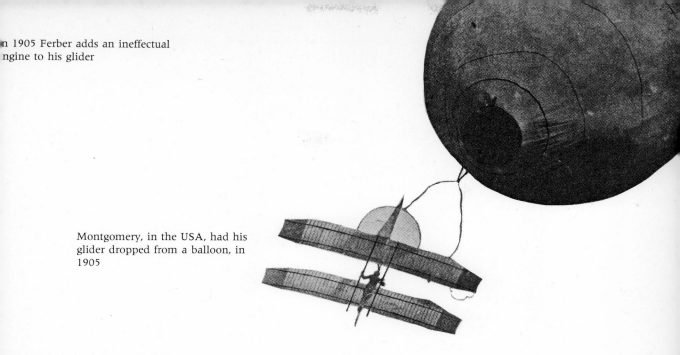

In 1905 Ferber adds an ineffectual engine to his glider

Montgomery, in the USA, had his glider dropped from a balloon, in 1905

In 1905 Cody, in England, built and flew this glider-kite

The Wright *Flyer III*, of 1905, the world's first practical aeroplane which could fly for half an hour and be banked, circled and flown in figures of eight. It was flown at the Huffman Prairie, near Dayton

A fine view of the Wrights' third powered Flyer banking over the flying ground near Dayton

A fine study of a white elephant,
Blériot's useless biplane of 1906

Vuia unsuccessfully starts the
monoplane tradition in France, 1906

Ellehammer in Denmark makes a
tethered semi-flight in 1906

Blériot just gets his tandem-wing
Libellule off the ground in 1907

Santos-Dumont, in France, tests his
tail-first biplane *14-bis* under his
airship in 1906 and then makes the
first hop-flights in Europe

In 1907 Blériot built his No. VII, a
tractor monoplane, which although
it was not itself successful, inspired
and set the style for future European
monoplanes

Ellehammer tests his triplane in
1907, the first full-scale machine of
its type

Santos-Dumont's unsuccessful No. 19
of 1907, the first light plane

Esnault-Pelterie with his first
powered monoplane, with wing-
warping, in 1907

De Pischoff in France tentatively
starts the tractor biplane tradition
in 1907

Voisin crystallises the European
pusher biplane type with this
unsuccessful machine in 1907

This slatted oddity by Phillips
managed to fly briefly in 1907

Farman flies the first circle in Europe
on his altered Voisin, 13 January
1908

Henri Farman on his altered Voisin
which he bought in 1907

The *Voisin-Delagrange* III (modified)
of 1908

Henri Farman, an Englishman living
in France, was the most famous
European pilot at this time. Here is
a fine study of his modified Voisin
biplane, but still a primitive machine
by the Wrights' standards: 1908

The Blériot VIII-*bis* of 1908 with
primitive ailerons fitted at the wing
ends

The start of a noble monoplane line,
designed by Levavasseur in 1908; the
Gastambide-Mengin I of 1908

The Curtiss *June Bug* makes a
brief public flight in the USA
in 1908: but it is still a
primitive machine

Santos-Dumont's little machine
in 1908, soon to develop into
the famous *Demoiselle*

It was Henri Farman who first learnt
the Wrights' lessons in flight-control
in 1908, and he added large ailerons
for roll control to his already much
modified Voisin biplane

An early unsuccessful triplane by
Goupy, 1908

The Grade triplane makes a wavering
flight in Germany, 1908

The Ellehammer IV biplane which
made some hop-flights in 1908

Roe's 1908 biplane which made some brief hop-flights at Brooklands

The Wright biplane which
revolutionised European flying by
its mastery of flight-control when
flown by Wilbur in France in 1908

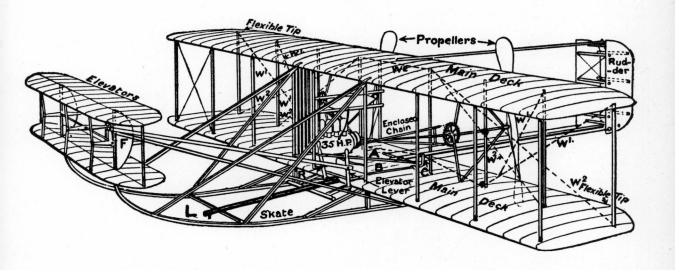

Labels on diagram: Flexible Tip, ←Propellers→, Rud--der, Elevators, Main Deck, W⁶, W¹, W², W², Enclosed Chain, 35 H.P., W¹, F, A, B, Elevator Lever, Main Deck, W², W²Flexible Tip, L, Skate, R

Wilbur Wright, on his standard
biplane, flying in France in 1908.
This highly sophisticated machine
is seen on the right exposed
diagrammatically. Control in pitch
was *via* the forward biplane elevator;
in yaw *via* the rear rudder; and in
roll *via* the warping of the wing
ends. All three controls could be
brought into action simultaneously
if necessary in any degree of
combination. This aircraft proved
a revelation to the slowly evolving
Europeans, and its flight-control set
the Continental pioneers on the right
road to success

The Wright biplane was catapulted off a monorail track laid into wind; but it could take off without this device if necessary. Soon after, small wheels were fitted to the skids. When women flew as passengers, their skirts had to be tied round with string to avoid both aerodynamic and moral hazards. On the right is one of the finest 'impressionistic' photos taken of the Wright aeroplane flying in France in 1908

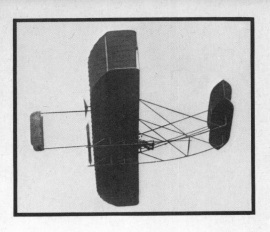

While Wilbur flew in France, Orville flew just as brilliantly in the US, but on 17 September 1908, a propeller broke and the resulting accident killed Orville's passenger, Lt Selfridge

On 16 October 1908, Cody made the first powered flight in Britain at Farnborough. Meanwhile, on the Continent in 1908, the Antoinette Company were building Levavasseur's graceful monoplanes, also called *Antoinettes*. Next year these aircraft were to mature into wonderful machines, as graceful as they were efficient

It was Orville who went to Berlin in
1909 to teach the Germans to fly
Wright machines

Orville Wright flying his machine in
Germany in 1909. The Germans were
at first behind in aviation

Cody's first powered aeroplane [see p. 104]

Portrait of a huge white elephant;
Dorand's multiplane (1908–9) which
never flew

The King of Spain was only allowed to sit with Wilbur on the aircraft, but not to fly with him

In January 1909 Wilbur Wright moved to Pau, in southern France, where he became a huge popular success

In 1909 Cody was the foremost
British pilot; he was naturalised in
this year

Esnault-Pelterie went on building his
monoplanes in 1909

Santos-Dumont's *Demoiselle* at last becomes a practical aeroplane in 1909

vaudan's freak aircraft which never w (1909)

In 1909, Roe flew his little triplanes;
the Canadian McCurdy flew the *Silver
Dart*; and Goupy piloted his prophetic
staggered-wing biplane in France

Hubert Latham in France became the
most famous pilot of the graceful
Antoinette monoplanes; and he was
first to attempt the Channel-crossing
in 1909

On 19 July 1909 Latham crashes at
his first attempt to cross the Channel

Louis Blériot was the second man to attempt the Channel crossing, and on 25 July 1909, he succeeded in this small but graceful Blériot No. XI, shown here in flight. He

was very lucky that the small 25 h.p. engine did not give up in this brave achievement; but it went on working and the Channel was crossed early in the morning

Here is the famous scene with Blériot
posing with spectators after he had
landed in a field near Dover Castle
on 25 July 1909

The Blériot XII, a 1909
monoplane which flew at Reims

Latham again tried to fly the
Channel in this *Antoinette* and
again failed, on 27 July 1909

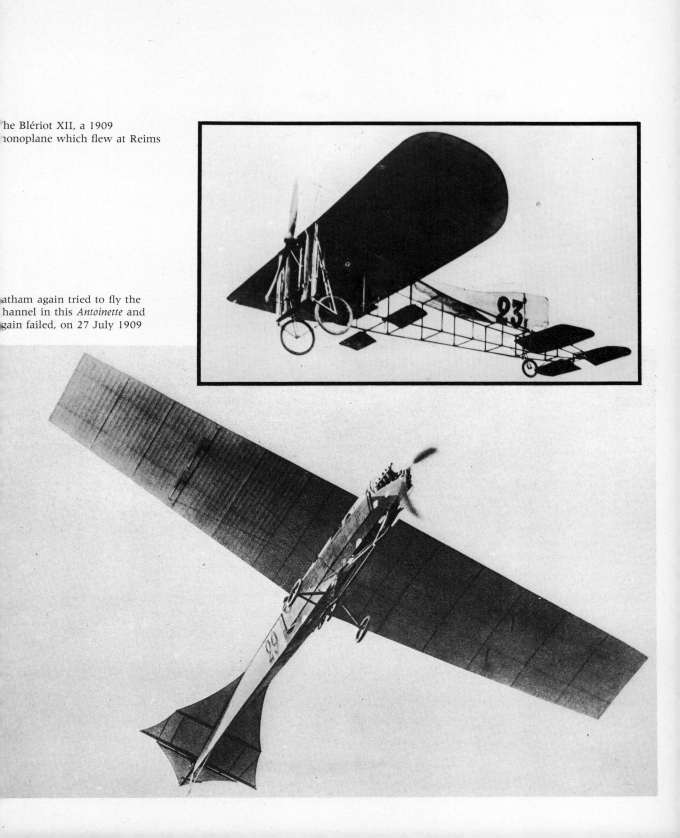

The First Aviation Meeting was held at Reims in 1909. Here is a Voisin biplane

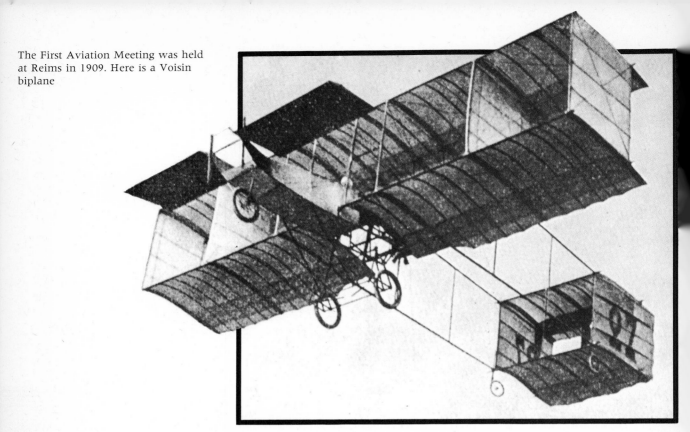

Although the Wrights did not attend the Reims meeting, some brilliant flying was done on Wright machines

The Henry Farman III biplane,
of the greatest machines of its

The Breguet biplane at Reims, 1909

Lefebvre flying his Wright biplane
brilliantly at Reims, here seen
rounding a pylon

Glenn Curtiss at Reims, where he won the main speed events